HOW THEY LIVED

A SCHOOLCHILD IN WORLD WAR II

MIRIAM MOSS

HOW THEY LIVED

An American Pioneer Family
An Australian Pioneer
An Aztec Warrior
A Celtic Family
A Sailor with Captain Cook
A Samurai Warrior
A Crusading Knight
An Edwardian Household
A Family in the Fifties
A Family in the Thirties
A Family in World War I
A Family in World War II
An Ice Age Hunter
An Inca Farmer
A Medieval Monk
A Medieval Serf
A Norman Baron

A Plains Indian Warrior
A Plantation Slave
A Roman Centurion
A Roman Gladiator
A Child in Victorian London
A Colonial American Merchant
A Saxon Farmer
A Schoolchild in World War II
A Slave in Ancient Greece
A Soldier in Wellington's Army
A Soldier in World War I
A Suffragette
A Teenager in the Sixties
A Tudor Merchant
A Victorian Factory Worker
A Viking Sailor

Editor: Amanda Earl

First Published in 1988 by
Wayland (Publishers) Limited
61 Western Road, Hove
East Sussex BN3 1JD, England

All words that appear in **bold**
in the text are explained
in the glossary on page 31.

British Library Cataloguing in Publication Data
Moss, Miriam
A schoolchild in World War II.
1. World War, 1939–1945 – Children –
Juvenile literature   2. Children – Great
Britain – History – 20th century –
Juvenile literature   3. Great Britain –
Social life and customs – 20th century –
Juvenile literature
I. Title   II. Series
941.084'088054   D810.C4
ISBN 1 85210 201 2

Typeset by Kalligraphics Limited, Redhill, Surrey.
Printed and bound in Belgium by Casterman S.A.

CONTENTS

WAR SOUVENIRS

Sally watched as one of the tiny specks far up in the blue sky started slowy spiralling to earth. She could see the flicker of flames around the engine and could pick out the German cross on the wings and **fuselage**. She looked in silence as it came down across the valley and crashed and exploded in the woods. Racing towards it, clutching her boxed **gas mask**, she prayed that she would not meet the **ARP warden** who would seal off the area. Then it would be impossible to add to her collection of **shrapnel**, spent bullets and other war souvenirs.

She began to smell smoke as she ran, but suddenly she stumbled and fell. Looking up, a few yards away she noticed an open wallet. Inside there was a photograph of a German soldier – what a war souvenir! Then she saw the tail of the crashed plane behind the trees . . .

World War II began in 1939 and lasted until 1945. This was perhaps when your grandparents were children. The war started because Adolf Hitler, the leader of the German people, attacked Poland. Britain and France were Poland's **allies** so they declared war on Germany. In time many countries became involved.

During the war millions of men, women and children died all over the world. Thousands of children were left homeless and many lost their parents. Children in Britain lived with the constant threat of a German invasion. They lived through frightening air raids and many town children were separated from their parents and **evacuated** to the country.

Thousands of children were made homeless by the bombing raids on major British cities during World War II.

Many German planes were shot down over Britain during the war.

5

PREPARATIONS FOR WAR

When war was declared, the British had some time to prepare as the Germans did not start bombing immediately. During the first two weeks, the government issued 500 instructions to help people get ready for war. Some leaflets explained how to stop light from escaping through windows at night by using heavy black curtains, or how to mask car headlights to cut down the light. Any light helped the German bombers

During the 'blackout', lampposts and curbs had to be painted white so people could see them.

find their targets more easily.

The blackout itself proved to be dangerous. Between September and November 1939, there were no deaths from air raids but 3,000 due to the blackout. People crashed their cars, broke their noses on street corners and chipped their teeth on lamp posts. Finally, the corners of houses and car mudguards were painted white to help stop these accidents.

Everyone was issued with a gas mask, in case of a gas attack. These had to be carried at all times. Babies had anti-gas helmets that were hand pumped. Toddlers had 'Donald Duck' masks and schoolchildren were fitted with standard civilian gas masks. Children did not like wearing them. One boy said his was 'all rubbery and nasty' and a girl said hers made her feel sick.

In 1939 many thousands of people bought air raid shelters. The simplest was a frame to put under the kitchen table. Others bought an Anderson shelter in kit form for £7. Children helped to dig a deep hole in the back garden. Six sheets of

Above *Even young children were issued with gas masks at the start of the war.*

Right *Air raid shelters were very small, but families (and their pets) made themselves as comfortable as possible!*

curved **corrugated steel** were put together to form a large arch. Two flat sheets of steel made up the ends, with a hole for the door. The shelter was then covered with about a metre of earth. These shelters could withstand anything but a direct hit. Inside there were bunks to sleep in, but in wet weather water often covered the earth floor. As the war continued families planted roses over the doorways of their shelters!

AIR RAID

The Blitz, the severe bombing of London and other major towns, began in September 1940 and lasted until May 1941. On hearing the wailing air raid **sirens** telling of the approaching bombers, children with their parents and school teachers, hurried into the air raid shelters. In London, the Underground Stations were used as shelters.

On one air raid, 300 German bombers approached London with twice as many fighter planes protecting them. The noise was deafening. High explosive bombs whistled and screamed finally crashing down with a terrifying sound. The **incendiary** bombs were quieter. They clattered as they rolled and rattled on rooftops and pavements; then there was a

Below *London children often sheltered in Underground Stations during an air raid.*

Below *During raids, new-born babies were moved from hospital to safer shelters.*

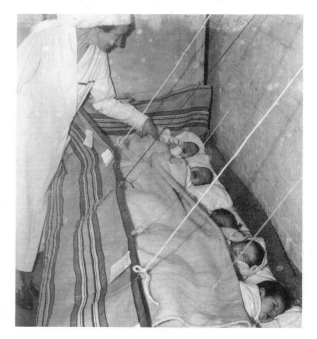

Huge 'doodlebugs' or V-1 bombs were fired by the Germans from the French coast.

silence as they began to burn. Later in the war, in 1944, children learned about a new threat from the skies. The Germans sent over **'doodlebugs'** and **V-2** rockets which caused great destruction.

When the 'All Clear' siren sounded children emerged to see the streets covered with glass from all the shattered windows, raging fires and buildings destroyed. One family returned home to find that half of their house had been blown away but that the kettle was still on the stove and the cups were still on the dresser!

Some people became used to spending hours in air raid shelters. In large shelters talent competitions were organized with prizes each week for the best singer or dancer. Everyone took pride in making sure that despite Hitler's bombs, life went on as normally as possible.

A father helps his son to rescue his bike from the ruins of their home.

EVACUATION

In September 1939 three and a half million children were moved from London and other big towns to the country, where they would be safe from the threat of German bombing. Half the children in London were evacuated. Some very young children were accompanied by their mothers but most went alone. They wore name tags and carried their gas masks.

They were assembled by their school teachers on station platforms and sent by train to the countryside. There they were met by a **billeting**

Thousands of children waited at train stations, ready for their evacuation.

Children arrive safely in the country. Some enjoyed their stay, others hated it.

officer. The host parents were given 8 shillings and sixpence (42p) a week by the government to feed and clothe each child.

The arrival of hundreds of children often caused chaos in the quiet country towns and villages. Country folk sometimes did not like the children because they had a different way of life and different manners.

They were often shocked by their poverty. Some children had lice in their hair or the skin disease **impetigo**. Many town children had never worn underpants before, wore no socks and had holes in their shoes. They were not used to eating fresh fruit and vegetables and asked for the tinned food or fish, chips and beer they were used to. Many felt miserably homesick and some children tried to run away. One child walked 48 km in the rain trying to get home.

The first evacuation scheme was a failure. Half the children had returned home by Christmas. These children returned to tell everyone what they had learned in the country – that horses were bigger than dogs and milk came from cows! After France was occupied by the Germans in 1940, the south and east coasts of England were heavily bombed and children were sent to more remote parts of the country, especially Wales. This was more successful as the government had learned from their mistakes.

When they were evacuated, city children had the chance to learn about country life.

FAMILY LIFE UNDER STRAIN

During the war thousands of fathers, brothers and uncles were called up to join the armed forces and were away for long periods. Unmarried women between the ages of 20 and 30 were also conscripted by the government to serve in the Auxiliary services. Many children spent many hours worrying about the safety of their relatives. They listened for news of the war abroad on the **wireless** and wrote letters, but these sometimes went astray. Many received telegrams saying that their relations were 'missing, presumed dead'.

News of the war was important to everybody, especially those with loved ones fighting.

Hundreds of children said goodbye to their fathers who were off to fight.

Many adults helped with the war effort at home by joining voluntary groups like the ARP or **Home Guard**. Relations in the the Home Guard trained after work, in the evenings and at weekends, so children often did not see much of them. Many women changed their jobs and went to work in munitions factories making bombs; others worked on farms. In industrial areas which were often bombed, children did not always go to school because of the sleepless nights spent in air raid shelters. Sometimes older

Adults did voluntary work during the war. This is an ARP warden.

Everybody in the family was encouraged to help in the war effort – even children.

children stayed at home to look after the youngsters because their mothers had war jobs.

The fear of losing a loved one made people behave differently. During the time of the worst daylight air raids many families kissed each other goodbye even if they were just going to the shops. The lack of time spent together as a family and the tiring voluntary work, put great strains on family life.

13

RATIONING

NOW—CAN I COVER MY TOES—OR BLOW MY NOSE?

It was difficult to provide enough food for everyone in Britain during the war. The life of the whole island depended on importing food in cargo ships and these were often sunk by German submarines.

Slowly rationing had to be introduced. Each person was given a ration book full of coupons that could be exchanged in the shops for food and clothing. Unfortunately the

A wartime postcard making lighthearted fun of rationing.

66 clothes coupons were often used up on one item. There was also a shoe shortage and many children stayed away from school when their only pair was being mended.

Many people found interesting and unusual ways of making small amounts of food go a long way and

14

some very strange foods were tried. Some children had to eat whale meat, boiled sheep's head and 'firewood sausages' which were made mainly of bread. Often young dandelion leaves were washed and used as lettuce, and stinging nettles were used in place of spinach!

Children were taught how to look after rabbits, feeding them so that they would grow fat on carrot tops and the outside leaves of cabbages. They were bred for their meat but some children found that they just could not eat the rabbits who had become their pets. Children kept hens too for their eggs and meat.

A typical week's supply of rationed food for one person during the war. Food was rationed differently at different times during the war, depending on supplies. Children and pregnant women received extra milk and eggs.

No food was wasted – even scraps were saved for farm animals!

Later, sweets were rationed and lucky children made friends with American soldiers (**GIs**) who gave them chewing gum. A famous saying was 'Got any gum, chum?'.

Birthday cakes looked different during the war as the government would not allow sugar to be put on the outside of any cake after baking. A fat child was a very rare sight during the war! Despite shortages and hardships many British children were far healthier at the end of the war because of their balanced diet.

15

DIGGING FOR VICTORY

During the war everyone was encouraged to stop growing flowers and to start growing vegetables, as German submarines continued to sink British food ships. If more food was produced at home sailors' lives could be saved. Growing food at home was called 'Digging for Victory'.

Children helped to turn large parks into allotments. At home they dug up lawns and turned them into vegetable plots. At school gardening sometimes replaced games as the chief outdoor exercise. No manure was available so they spread ashes and soot over the soil. Even the

Left *Everybody was encouraged to grow their own food, as this poster shows.*

Below *These children with their mother proudly display home-grown vegetables.*

DIG FOR VICTORY

For their sake-
GROW YOUR OWN VEGETABLES

window boxes and the ornamental tubs outside London's West End clubs had tomatoes growing in them!

The government asked the children to 'lend a hand on the land' as many farmers were short of helpers. Their usual workers had been called up to fight. They were even released from school for 'potato picking' weeks. By 1943, about 470,000 schoolchildren were helping on the land. There were also more than 150 camps of volunteers in which two-thirds were women. These volunteers gave up their jobs to help the farmers. They were called Land Girls or the Women's Land Army.

Above *A little girl prepares a trellis for her runner beans on Hampstead Heath, London.*

Below *During harvest time, children volunteered to 'lend a hand on the land'.*

RECREATION

Children growing up between 1939 and 1945 lived and breathed the war. It captured their imaginations while they played at home and at school. They pretended to be German and British planes fighting. The local children were the 'Spitfires' and the evacuees were the 'enemy bombers'. Girls skipped to rhymes about Hitler and Churchill (the British leader), while other children played 'desert warfare' on blitzed sites.

They were divided into the

Children enjoyed playing war games and dressing up as soldiers.

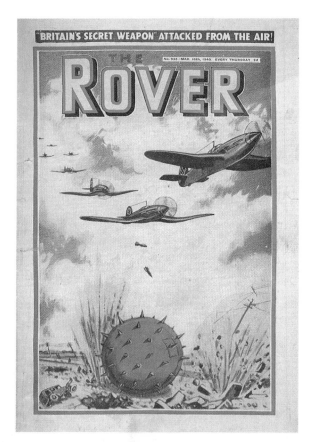

Comics such as the Rover *and* Hotspur *included many wartime adventure stories.*

German Afrika Korps and the British 8th Army. They threw sand and other missiles from the site at each other to make the enemy's army retreat. Children played games about British agents in Germany and about identifying German spies in Britain.

Children made up special games to play during the blackout. One was called 'blackout bump' where the children tried to crawl on their hands and knees to a particular spot without bumping into each other. In another game a child wearing a gas mask stuck his or her head through a hole in a sheet while the others tried to guess who it was.

One favourite activity for older children was aircraft spotting using the sixpenny (3p) Penguin book of aircraft silhouettes or the weekly issue of the *Aircraft Spotter* to help with identification. Gangs of school children toured the countryside on their bikes, hoping to find war souvenirs. German pilots' helmets, pieces of German aircraft or the tail fins of bombs were treasured.

Children enjoyed going to the cinema to watch films like 'Goodbye Mr Chips' or cartoons starring Mickey Mouse, Donald Duck and Pluto. They also liked listening to the BBC Home Service programmes on the wireless. Many children wrote in to Sandy Macpherson who had a programme called 'Sandy's Half Hour'. He played musical requests on the organ for the Forces and their families.

As a special treat during the war, children's parties were sometimes arranged with all kinds of jelly and cakes.

WAR TOYS

During the early part of the war there was a flood of military toys, like imitation steel helmets and rifles, clockwork tanks, model **barrage balloons** and Red Cross nurses' uniforms. Children enjoyed playing with toy bombs. They were on a string holding a cap which exploded with a loud crack when it was dropped. Large whistles were also popular which made a siren-like noise. When they were connected to a blown-up balloon they sounded like the 'All Clear' siren.

A board game for two players called 'GHQ' had armoured, motorized and **infantry** divisions which fought each other across a map of Europe. One firm replaced the Happy Families characters in the card game with bombers and fighters and called the cards 'War Planes'.

Below left *Military toys were very popular during the war.*

Below *Dolls dressed in Navy and Army uniforms were found in larger shops.*

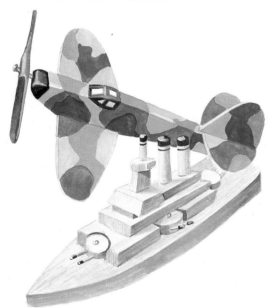

As the war continued, toys became very scarce. This doll's house was made from a birdcage.

By 1941 toy factories had changed over to making supplies for the war, so most toys had vanished from the shops. Parents had to become very resourceful at Christmas – one parent made a doll's house out of an old birdcage. Bits of cardboard were used for the walls, an old office file for the roof, dyed hessian pieces for the carpets and tiny pictures were made out of cigarette cards.

School toy-making clubs made jigsaws from pictures glued on to pieces of plywood. Rag dolls with button-eyes were made from old stockings and coats were converted into stuffed animals. Some toys were very simple: 'whizzers' were made out of cardboard, milk bottle tops and large buttons. These whizzed when their supporting strings were jerked tight. Doorknobs were used as yo-yos and cowboy outfits were made from curtain lining and a lamp-shade fringe.

At Christmas, Americans sent presents to hundreds of bomb-victim families and evacuated children in Britain.

THE CROWDED CLASSROOM

World War II was a very interesting and eventful time for children at school but a great headache for teachers. There was a shortage of teachers as many were called up or sent to help with war duties elsewhere. Classrooms with 50 or 60 children in them were not unusual. In some village schools a single classroom held children aged from 5 to 14. There were too many pupils and not enough books and equipment. Children sometimes had to share pencils and there was also a great shortage of paper. Margins were abolished and every millimetre of space was used.

School lessons were held in very strange places, including some stately homes.

Thirty-four children died in the daylight raid on this school.

Some were held in hotels and even pubs! Children were taught in the village church or down in the church **crypt**. Sometimes gym lessons were held between rows of coats in the cloakroom.

After the first evacuation of children many schools were made into defence depots or fire stations. By January 1940 this meant that one-third of all the children in the cities were receiving no education at all. In evacuated areas 'home schools' were common where a group of children met for two mornings a week in someone's house.

The children wrote compositions about what they would do to Hitler if they caught him and about how happy they would be when their fathers got home. As part of their lessons they also followed the troop movements in Europe on a big *Daily Telegraph* map, locating where ships had been sunk.

Thousands of schools were hit by bombs and partly or wholly destroyed. As a result, classes were held in some very strange places.

Evacuated children were often taught at home.

SCHOOLS UNDER FIRE

During the war there were some daylight air raids on schools and many children died tragically. Teachers and children practised wearing gas masks and getting to the air raid shelter. When the siren went each class marched quickly across the playground to the shelter. They carried their gas masks, a wad of cotton wool to plug their ears, a big clean handkerchief to use as a bandage in case of an emergency and they wore a name tag.

Inside the shelter there were wooden benches and caged lights on the walls. Each child had a tin or box in which they kept two or three comics, a book, some sweets and a favourite toy to keep them occupied.

'Alerts' at night were popular with the children because if it sounded before midnight, morning school was postponed for one hour. Exams were often interrupted by the siren sounding the alert, and one teacher turned round from the blackboard to see that her class had completely vanished. They had heard a doodlebug and had dived under their desks!

Schoolchildren cleared their games pitches of bomb splinters and cartridge cases before each game. Bombs weighing 22 kg were found in fields and playgrounds and made huge craters. It was a very worrying time for parents as school buses and

Children look at the terrible damage caused by a bomb to their school playground. Boxed gas masks, like the girl's on the left, should have been carried at all times.

Above *To keep themselves amused in the school shelter, children were allowed to read their favourite comic.*

Right *A child bomb victim is carried to safety by an ARP warden.*

trains were occasionally machine gunned by German planes. Parents hated having to sew name tapes on their children's school uniforms so that they could be identified should they be killed by a bomb.

25

CLUBS AND VOLUNTEERS

Many children helped with the war effort by joining youth organizations. The numbers of children joining Cubs, Brownies, Guides and Scouts rose quickly during the war years. The Girl Guides and the Boy Scouts had a million members between them. Often there was a shortage of adults to run the groups and finding halls to meet in was difficult.

The kind of help that these young people offered was often the hard work behind the scenes in an emergency. They brewed the tea at reception centres for the wounded, checked and refilled fire buckets and tested **stirrup pumps** at local hospitals. They also helped to prepare the supper for hospital patients twice a week. The War Service Badge was awarded to Girl Guides for doing a certain number of hours of hospital work, gardening and running messages each year.

Girl Guides collect messages to deliver to different government offices. The Guides also raised £50,000 of funds during the war which helped to buy 20 new ambulances.

Youth organizations also helped by making collections of silver paper, scrap iron and pots and pans which were all recycled to make aeroplanes and munitions. They even collected cotton reels for the Army signallers to wind thin wires around and use as part of their equipment.

In December 1941 all young people, on reaching the age of 16,

By 1944, the Boy Scouts had 452,000 members helping with the war effort.

When they reached 18, youths were old enough to join one of the services. The ATS was the women's Auxiliary Territorial Service.

were given advice about joining a suitable youth organization. The Air Training Corps gave early training to those who wanted to join the RAF when they were old enough, while the Girl's Training Corps gave training in signalling and drill.

27

PROPAGANDA AND RUMOURS

The government wanted to keep up people's spirits during the war and so they issued posters with messages on them. Children shopping in Woolworth's saw large, bright red posters displaying the message 'Your Courage, Your Cheerfulness, Your Resolution, Will Bring Us Victory'. Children would have seen this **propaganda** throughout the war on hoardings, in trains and at food depots.

In 1940 people were fined £50 if they passed on a rumour likely to

Below left *Posters urging people to 'keep their spirits up' were seen everywhere.*

Below *During the war people were told not to gossip, as this poster shows.*

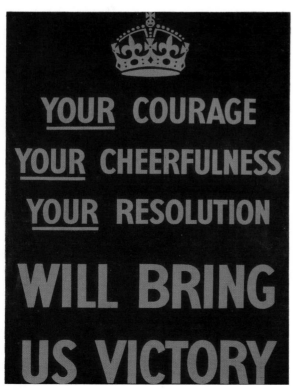

"…. strictly between these four walls!"

CARELESS TALK COSTS LIVES

you never know who's listening!

CARELESS TALK COSTS LIVES

Above and above right *The famous 'Careless talk costs lives' posters. Can you see Hitler and Goering?*

cause 'alarm and despondency'. Children were encouraged to 'Join the Silent Column' and not to spread rumours. Even newspapers printed articles urging people to avoid gossiping.

There was also a government campaign against giving information to the enemy. Slogans appeared warning children that 'Careless talk costs lives', and that 'Walls have ears'. One cartoon enjoyed by children was two women gossiping on a bus with Hitler and Goering sitting behind them. The caption read 'You never know who's listening'.

VICTORY!

On 8 May 1945, the day that the war in Europe was over, there were all sorts of celebrations. It was the happiest day that many children could remember. There was singing, dancing, cheering and street parties. There were banners and balloons everywhere and the celebrations went on for many days. Even babies became part of the celebrations.

The war had brought with it many changes for children – fewer sweets, no new clothes and disrupted schooling. Yet, it did succeed in bringing adults and children much closer to each other than ever before, as families suffered losses and hardships together. It is very sad to think that more children died in World War II than in all the previous wars in the world for a 100 years.

For most children World War II was a mixture of exciting times and sad times.

On VE day (Victory in Europe) on 8 May 1945 celebrations went on into the night. Imagine the joy and relief felt by everybody after nearly six years at war.

GLOSSARY

Allies Countries fighting on the same side in war.

ARP Warden An Air Raid Precaution official.

Barrage balloon A balloon made of rubber proofed cotton, filled with hydrogen. It was supposed to stop enemy aircraft.

Billeting officer Someone in charge of organizing where people are to live.

Corrugated steel Sheets of steel with ridges for the rain to run down.

Crypt Underground chamber or cellar.

Doodlebug Another name for the V-1, a 'robot' bomb invented by the Germans.

Evacuated Taken away from a place of danger to a place of safety.

Fuselage The main body of an aircraft.

Gas mask A mask fitted with a chemical filter which allows the wearer to breathe air free of poisonous gases.

GIs A slang term for American soldiers. GI stands for 'government issue'.

Home Guard An unpaid force who were trained to protect the country in case of invasion.

Impetigo A skin disease which is very catching.

Incendiary A bomb which exploded into flames when it hit the ground.

Infantry Soldiers who fight on foot.

Propaganda An organized way of spreading a particular belief or view.

Shrapnel Fragments of explosive shells or bombs.

Sirens Devices which give out a loud wailing sound, used to warn people of an air raid attack.

Stirrup pump A hand operated pump used to fight fires. The base of the cylinder-shaped pump is placed in a bucket of water.

V-2 A rocket powered bomb used by the Germans to bombard London.

Wireless Another word for a radio.

MORE BOOKS TO READ

Robert Hoare, *World War Two* (Macdonald, 1973)

Michael Hobbs, *One Day in World War II* (Robert Tyndall Ltd, 1974)

Kathleen Monham, *Growing up in World War II* (Wayland, 1979)

Stewart Ross, *A Family in World War II* (Wayland, 1985)

INDEX

Picture acknowledgements
The pictures in this book were supplied by the following: BBC Hulton Picture Library 6, 7 (above), 9 (below), 10, 12 (above), 13 (left), 16 (right), 17 (above), 20 (right), 23 (above), 30; The Bridgeman Art Library 9 (above), 15, (right); The Girl Guides Association 26; Imperial War Museum 16 (left), 27 (right); John Frost Pictures 18 (right), 25 (left); Mary Evans Picture Library 13 (right), 29 (right); TOPHAM 4, 7 (below), 8 (both), 11 (both), 12 (below), 14, 15 (left), 17 (below), 18 (left), 19, 21, 22, 23 (below), 24, 25 (right), 28 (both), 29 (left). The artwork on page 5 is by Mark Bergin and the artwork on pages 20 and 21 is by Paul Jordan.